POPE JOHN PAUL II
AN AMERICAN CELEBRATION

"Let us thank God for the extraordinary human epic that is the United States of America."

Pope John Paul II, Cathedral of the Sacred Heart,
Newark, New Jersey, October 4, 1995.

FOREWORD BY
ARCHBISHOP THEODORE McCARRICK

THE HISTORIC U.S. VISIT AS DOCUMENTED BY THE JERSEY PHOTOGRAPHIC PROJECT

E l f
Publishing, Inc.

Pope John Paul II An American Celebration

Library of Congress Catalog Card Number: 95-061791
ISBN: 0-9647000-9-3
Printed in the United States of America

For extra copies of this book please check with your local bookstore, or write:
Elf Publishing, Inc.
385 Catherine St.
Somerville, NJ 08876
or call 908-231-9392.

Contents

Acknowledgments:

Editor and publisher:
Loren Fisher

Photographers:
Beth Balbierz
David P. Bergeland
Walter Choroszewski
Dean Curtis
J. M. Eddins, Jr.
Loren Fisher
Jim Graham
Alan Petersime
John Severson
Carl Walsh

Writers:
Robin Gaby Fisher
Neva Rae Fox
Jill Vejnoska

Photo editors:
Brian Horton
Alan Petersime
Loren Fisher

Content editor:
Lilah Lohr

Design and layout:
Loren Fisher

Printing and color separations by Nittany Valley Offset, State College, Pa.

On the cover: Pope John Paul II during Mass at Baltimore's Oriole Park at Camden Yards.

PHOTO BY DEAN CURTIS

"Hey, let's do a book on the pope." Originally, it was a little like Spanky and Our Gang putting on a show. It sounded like a great idea but I knew it would take the help of many people and this is my feeble attempt to thank all of you.

Putting together a project like this is a daunting task. I drew a lot of strength from Robin Gaby Fisher, my wife and best friend. Her constant support and encouragement got me through the tough times.

Early on, there were times when I was ready to give up. Each time that happened I would remember Jim Valvano, the former North Carolina State basketball coach who died of cancer a couple of years ago. While terminally ill, Valvano received an award on TV. Barely able to get to the podium, he delivered a powerful speech and implored "Don't give up, don't ever give up." I repeated those words out loud on many occasions. My thanks to Valvano for touching me and, I'm sure, so many others.

Many thanks to the marvelous photographers, writers and editors who worked on the project. Special thanks to David Bergeland for making all the color prints; Dean and Cindy Curtis and Alan Petersime for being there.

Michael Hurley, Communications Director for the Archdiocese of Newark, provided an incredible amount of support and assistance. Without his help, this book would not have been produced. I'm still not sure, but I have a feeling he is the main reason we were able to get a photographer aboard the papal plane from Rome.

Thanks also to Regina Bishop, Marie Kruzan, John Mailhot, Marianne Timmons, Mary Jo Patterson, Penny Zucheri, Courier-News friends Ed Pagliarini, Leo Hsu, Ed Murray, Kathy Johnson, Pasquale DiFulco and Linda Dexheimer.

Peter Stanton and Denise Rossitto of Stanton Communications, Msgr. Francis Maniscalco and Sister Mary Ann Walsh of the U.S. Catholic Conference, Bill Blaul of the Archdiocese of Baltimore and Vik van Brantegem of the Holy See Press Office.

Fern and Barry Sheinmel and Lorine Bruckmeyer-Weinstein at Moto Photo in Raritan, N.J. for their great film processing and fast service. Lorine even spent one night sleeping on the lab floor because we didn't get film there on time.

Steve Artz for repairing a big lens in the middle of the night, Bob Fishkin of Fishkin Bros. in Perth Amboy, N.J. Glen Jasionowski and Frank Illuzzi at Unique Photo in Orange, N.J. and Marc Freund of Photo Systems, Inc., Dexter, Mich, for their donation of film. Laura Italiano of New Jersey Online, Bill Pekela, Gail and Jill at Nikon Pro Services, Joe Delora at Canon Pro Services, Debra Talbot and the crew at Nittany Valley Offset.

Thanks to our support team of Sarah Fisher and Jesse May who endured much of the same hours as the rest of the team but don't get to see their hard work in print.

Finally, thanks to Sarah and Louis Fisher for their constant support, work and love.

There were many highs and one significant low. Writer Neva Rae Fox and photographer Carl Walsh had the chance to kiss the Holy Father's ring while he was at Baltimore's Basilica. Both were thrilled beyond belief. But one photographer, Jim Graham, had his bag full of cameras stolen while we were standing around a hotel lobby. Jim rebounded to make the best picture I have seen of the visit (see pages 8-9). Prints of that photo and four others are available (see page 128). Maybe we can help him pay for some of that equipment.

The Jersey Photographic Project team

Beth Balbierz

Originally from Grand Rapids, Mich., Beth worked at newspapers in Indiana and Michigan after receiving a journalism degree from Michigan State University. Since moving to New Jersey, Beth has freelanced and now is a part-time photographer for The Record in Hackensack. She and her husband, Rob, have been married four years and have an infant daughter, Samantha.

David P. Bergeland

In 1984, Dave started working for daily newspapers as a photojournalist in Aberdeen, S.D. after receiving a BS in Agriculture and Economics from South Dakota State University. Following his work at the Argus Leader in Sioux Falls, S.D., Dave moved to the East Coast to work with photo editor Loren Fisher for over six years. During this time, he helped create The Jersey Photographic Project with Fisher, which helped his career expand into commercial work and book publishing. Currently, Bergeland, 33, is working for the Asbury Park Press in Neptune, N.J.

Dean Curtis, wearing vest, gets off the papal plane.

PHOTO BY ALAN PETERSIME

Walter Choroszewski

Best known for his colorful portrayals of New Jersey and the Mid-Atlantic states, Walter is a photographic artist who has produced numerous books and calendars over the last 15 years. His images have been widely published — from the New Jersey State Tourism promotions to Bell Atlantic's telephone directories, as well as in many other advertising, editorial, and corporate publications. A native of Pennsylvania and graduate of Penn State University, Walter started his career in photography in New York City before moving to New Jersey in 1986. He and his family currently reside in Somerset County, N.J.

Dean Curtis

Photo editor at the Springfield News-Leader in Springfield, Mo., Dean, 36, is a national award winning photographer. He worked at newspapers in North Dakota, South Dakota and New Jersey before moving to Springfield with his wife, Cindy, and son, Andy, 3, in 1992. They are expecting another child in April of 1996. Dean has been a photojournalist for 13 years and has been published in numerous national publications. His work appears in the book, "Branson Backstage" also by Elf Publishing.

Joe Eddins, Jr.

A staff photographer for Patuxent Publishing, a chain of 11 Baltimore, Md., suburban weekly newspapers, Joe graduated from West Virginia University in 1984 with a BA in Journalism and minors in English, political science and banjo-picking. He was sports editor and staff photographer for The Record in Havre de Grace, Md., from 1985 to 1989.

Loren Fisher

President of Elf Publishing, Inc., Loren is co-founder of The Jersey Photographic Project. After graduating from Ball State University in Muncie, Ind., Loren worked as a photographer and editor for newspapers in Indiana, Ohio and New Jersey. His first book, "Branson Backstage" was published in August, 1995. He lives in Somerville, N.J. with his wife, Robin Gaby Fisher, two cats and Bandit the watch dog.

Robin Gaby Fisher

A general assignment writer for The Star-Ledger in Newark, New Jersey's leading newspaper, Robin has covered numerous events involving high-ranking officials, including Presidents Reagan, Bush and Clinton. None have personally moved her like the pope's visit to America. The recipient of numerous writing awards, Robin lives with her husband, Loren, two cats and Bandit, the watchdog, in Somerville, N.J.

Neva Rae Fox

A former newspaper reporter and editor for Times-Graphics Newspapers in N.J., Neva entered the public relations world and is currently director of public relations activities for Dana Communications, a national agency in New Jersey. Her articles have been published in national and state magazines, and she has earned five professional awards. The editor of her statewide diocesan newspaper and a contributor to local and area social causes, Neva resides in Somerville, NJ, with her husband and two cats.

Jim Graham

A freelance photographer based in

Jim Graham waits for the pope's Baltimore arrival.

PHOTO BY ALAN PETERSIME

Wilmington, Del., Jim specializes in editorial and commercial photography. Jim worked for 13 years at the Wilmington News-Journal where he was nominated for the Pulitzer Prize in News Photography and won Southern Photographer of the Year (1990). Jim graduated from Washington College in 1981 with a bachelor's degree in history and has attended the Missouri Workshop and the resident program of the Maine Photographic Workshop.

Alan Petersime

Photo editor since 1986 for the Chronicle-Tribune in Marion, Ind., and staff photographer for the two prior years, Alan previously worked for the Jasper, Ind., Herald and the Wabash, Ind. Plain Dealer. He has won the Indiana Photographer of the Year, the John Alhauser

Understanding Award and the Gannett Black & White Photographer of the Year. He and his wife Janet have two children, Hannah, 10, and Zach, 6, plus a dog, cat, rabbit and fish. He favors green M&Ms.

John Severson

A staff photographer at the News-Press in Fort Myers, Fla. since 1987, Severson, 44, previously worked at newspapers in Indiana and Michigan. A Wisconsin native, John graduated from Luther College in Decorah, Iowa with a B.A. in accounting and business. He is a self-taught photographer with experience in studio and freelance work. This is not John's first pope sighting. During his younger years, while traveling in Europe, John joined an audience at the Vatican where he not only saw His Holiness, but got a picture with his first cam-

era, a Kodak point & shoot. Unfortunately, he is unable to recall which pope he saw.

Jill Vejnoska

A newspaper reporter for nine years, Jill currently covers politics and government for the Atlanta Journal-Constitution. Prior to moving to Georgia, she worked for USA Today and the Bridgewater, N.J., Courier News, where she won the 1989 "Best of Gannett" award for news reporting. Jill received an English degree from Harvard University and a master's in journalism from Columbia University.

Carl Walsh

Based in Biddeford, Me., Carl works as a freelance photographer. He is currently shooting a series of children's books about people living normal lives despite various diseases. He traveled to Madagascar last summer to start work on a project about an indigenous culture. Formerly Carl was a staff photographer at the Journal Tribune in Biddeford where, between 1988 and 1990, he was three-time New England Press Photographer of the Year. Last year was the third year in a row Carl has been runner up for that title.

Foreword

Most Reverend
Theodore E. McCarrick
Archbishop of Newark

Most Reverend Theodore E. McCarrick, Archbishop of Newark, during prayer service at Sacred Heart Cathedral.

PHOTO BY LOREN FISHER

When Time Magazine selected Pope John Paul II as its Man of the Year last January, it came as no surprise to the millions of people, Catholic and non-Catholic alike, who have been following the fascinating and historic events in the Holy Father's life: as a courageous survivor of the harassment of the Polish Catholic Church under both Nazis and communists, as one of the youngest bishops in Europe at the time of his consecration, as an influential voice in the deliberations of the Second Vatican Council, and as the first non-Italian to be elected to the Papacy in four centuries. Karol Wojtyla must be a figure of extraordinary importance in the world of the 20th century.

Even as a philosopher, John Paul II has had a strong impact on modern intellectuals who follow the schools of personalism and phenomenology. If he had not been elected Bishop of Rome in 1978, his philosophical writings may well have earned him recognition as one of the most important Catholic thinkers of this half of the century. As a poet, a dramatist and a scholar, his work with its profound analysis of life and faith in the context of our society has made its own contribution to the fields of art and science.

Perhaps more than any of the foregoing, I believe the Holy Father has made the deepest impression on today's world through his special charisma of relating to people of every age, race and way of life, this gift which the Spanish call "el don de gente" — the gift for people. The Pope seems to be at home within the academic circles of western culture as well as with the most uneducated people of an undeveloped country, with farmers and doctors, with invalids and athletes, with young and old. If there is any group with whom this charisma is most apparent it is in his dealing with youth. As he grows older, this ability seems all the more prominent, as we have seen so markedly in Denver and Manila.

Following pages, Pope John Paul II prays at the Basilica of the Assumption in Baltimore.

PHOTO BY JIM GRAHAM

As we celebrate the Pope's fourth major visit to our country, we are conscious of the personality of the man as well as the significance of his office. We Catholics see in John Paul II the successor of St. Peter to whom the Lord gave the keys of the kingdom, the power and the responsibility to lead the Church as teacher and shepherd. As the number of baptized Catholics in the world today reaches one billion souls, the enormous burden on his shoulders is evident. He has never flinched from what he likes to call his Petrine Function, his care of all the people of God.

His voice has been raised against the evils of atheistic communism as well as against the evils of depersonalizing capitalism. He has been a voice for the poor, the persecuted, the marginalized, the victims of war in every area of the world. His second visit to the United Nations, a body to which he has given the great support of his moral authority, is a milestone in the life of that organization. He has spoken out forcefully in defense of the values of human life and of family,

taking on fearlessly the enemies of those precious concepts wherever he finds them, whether in the halls of government or in the control rooms of the media or in the offices of the rich and powerful.

His visit to our country comes at a time of great expectation for the Catholic Church in the United States. A short time ago, Pope John Paul II presented to the church and to the world his apostolic letter on the third millennium. This has become a dominant theme in the Holy Father's talks and messages as he looks forward to the year 2000 with a palpable optimism and hope. He is determined to galvanize the whole church in every continent to prepare for this significant year. The preparation will, of course, be primarily spiritual. It must include the recognition of the past weaknesses and faults of the church seen as a human instrument, and therefore must strive to undo the harm that religious division has caused in the past 1,000 years. A genuine spirit of ecumenism and interreligious cooperation is very much

in the mind and very often on the lips of the Pontiff.

To New Jersey, in a particular way, this visit was a time of grace. Often sandwiched in between large states and more popular cities, we here in the Garden State welcomed the Holy Father with great joy. There are more than three million Catholics in this state and all are conscious of the fact that the Pope made a special effort to visit us. His arrival at Newark International Airport, his visit to pray in Sacred Heart Cathedral and the great Mass in Giants Stadium were followed carefully and with real interest by our own faithful and by our neighbors who know the central role which the Holy Father plays in our religious lives.

During these five historic days in October, as the third millennium looms in sight, as the eyes of the world focused on the United Nations and this special guest, we looked with gratitude and affection to John Paul II as he came as a pilgrim to pray in our churches and to speak to us personally and powerfully of the things of God.

"You young people will live most of your lives in the next millennium. You must help the Holy Spirit to shape its social, moral and spiritual character."

Pope John Paul II, Central Park, New York, New York, October 7, 1995.

First they hoped and prayed for tickets, and then — one uphill battle won — they scaled snaking, sloping streets for the right to stand in a field full of mud, their view diminished by the backs of too many others' heads.

Even people with the "best" spots — those who had risen with the sun before it turned traitorously hot in autumn — seemed uncertain of their good fortune.

Were they closest to everything, or farthest away?

Would something happen very soon, or was the waiting never to end?

Was this what was meant by having faith?

Suddenly there was a far-off rumble, and as it grew in intensity and proximity, 20,000 pairs of eyes shot up towards the heavens.

"Here he comes!"

The screams began even before the Marine Blackhawk helicopter swung into view, and thousands of people started clapping and crying and racing toward where it likely would touch down just beyond this rolling field behind St. Joseph's Seminary in Yonkers.

"He's coming!"

For five days in October of 1995, there was no need to ask who "he" was. Know that he was beloved.

In Newark, N.J., people who were decked out as elegantly as the soaring French gothic Sacred Heart Cathedral, where they attended Vespers services, perched perilously on top of pews and shouted without reserve: "Viva Papa!" ... "Viva Papa!" Long live the Pope!

It was that way everywhere he went.

Outside St. Patrick's Cathedral in New York City, where the pope was leading a rosary service, impromptu chants of "John Paul II, we love you!" broke out. In Giants Stadium, 83,000 people waited for four hours in lashing rain to celebrate Mass with him. In Sacred Heart Cathedral, cloistered nuns seemed to tremble as the pontiff approached them, then exhorted him: "Touch my hand!" In a Baltimore soup kitchen, a little girl hugged her new "Uncle Pope."

The 75-year-old Pope visited three states on this, his fourth tour of the United States. Admission to his services was so fiercely sought after that dozens of Catholic churches more accustomed to running bingo games suddenly found themselves

conducting ticket lotteries. Those who were lucky enough to come up with winning tickets were facing the largest security contingent ever amassed to protect a visiting head of state, and one which played no favorites. At Sacred Heart Cathedral, for instance, nearly a dozen cardinals were stopped at a side door by grim-faced Secret

Service agents who ran metal detectors over every inch of their brilliantly colored silk cassocks.

Across the street from the cathedral, meanwhile, thousands of non-ticket holders continued their

tures that greeted those staking out early prime spots along the Baltimore route of the first-ever papal parade.

Yet the hundreds of thousands who turned out at every city on the pon-

York City at 4:30 in the morning, she knew she would never get into the area known as the Great Lawn, where 125,000 ticketholders attended the Mass.

"I can't see the pope, but

Pope John Paul II is greeted as he enters Newark's Cathedral of the Sacred Heart.

PHOTO BY ALAN PETERSIME

hours-long wait in unpredictable weather extremes: driving rain and swirling winds during a nighttime mass at Giants Stadium in New Jersey; searing heat that felled some 150 people during an outdoor mass at New York's Aqueduct Racetrack; brisk tempera-

tiff's tour seemed willing to wait as long as it took just to be able to say they'd seen Pope John Paul II. Or at least felt his presence.

Gloria DiRaimo left Rhode Island in the middle of the night for the pontiff's Central Park Mass. Even though she arrived in New

once he starts saying the Mass, you'll feel him," she insisted. "I can hear, and that's all that counts. Everyone can't be in the front pew."

So many had waited a lifetime for this moment. A lifetime, plus one year.

Twelve months ago, jubilation greeted the Vatican's announcement that John Paul II would visit New Jersey and Baltimore — where no pontiff had ever been — and New York, where he'd been enthusiastically embraced in 1979 on his first American tour.

Delight turned to disappointment when the 1994 tour was canceled because of the Pope's slow recovery from hip replacement surgery.

But John Paul II was determined to reschedule. When he made good on that promise one year later, it only endeared him more to the millions of Americans — Catholics and otherwise — who see him as a truly holy man, but also as a truly human man.

Born in Poland in 1920, Karol Joseph Wojtyla lost his mother and older brother by the age of 12. In 1941, his father died, leaving him alone; in 1942, he began secretly studying for the priesthood at an underground seminary in Nazi-occupied Krakow and helped smuggle Jews out of Poland.

Despite being blacklisted by the Nazis, Wojtyla pursued his seminary studies and was ordained in 1946. Yet, the post-World War II Poland in which he began priesthood soon fell under communist rule. His academic and clerical career was brilliant, but it wasn't until 1964, when Poland's communist government lifted its ban on certain religious appointments, that Wojtyla could be named an archbishop.

Within three years he was inducted into the College of Cardinals. A decade later, his election as pope came as a huge surprise to the worldwide Catholic community, long accustomed to having Italians occupy

Pope John Paul II during Mass at Giants Stadium.

PHOTO BY LOREN FISHER

St. Peter's throne.

Even more startling was the forcefulness of his personality. The 58-year-old Wojtyla took the name John Paul II - and the world by storm. No other pope had traveled as much or with so much obvious zest for human contact as John Paul II. During his first visit here in 1979, millions of supposedly jaded Americans bought John Paul II t-shirts and baseball caps, and waited up to ten hours on city streets to try to touch him as he glided by in his open-air popemobile.

A would-be assassin's bullet nearly ended the pope's life in 1981, and severely curtailed the public's access to him. Still, the man who had refused to buckle under Nazism and communism refused to retreat from the shadow of political extremism to the comfort and security of the Vatican. He quickly resumed touring and meeting with such controversial figures as PLO leader Yasser Arafat as part of his quest for world peace. And, during an extraordinary visit to an Italian prison cell, he even made peace with the man who had tried to kill him.

John Paul II stepped off "Shepherd I" at Newark International Airport on Oct. 4, 1995, in his simple white cassock, a towering figure of power and compassion. Beginning an hour later, at Sacred Heart Cathedral, and continuing for the next five days, his overall message was the same: "Be not afraid." Of pursuing one's faith; of comforting the poor and the sick; of making the sacrifices necessary to serve God as a priest or nun.

Or of cherishing five awe-inspiring days in October.

• • •

Pope John Paul II's itinerary

Wednesday, October 4, 1995
3 pm Arrival at Newark International Airport, Newark, N.J.
5 pm Evening Prayer at Sacred Heart Cathedral, Newark, N.J.

Thursday, October 5, 1995
9:15 am Visit and addresses to the United Nations, New York, N.Y.
6 pm Celebration of Mass at Giants Stadium, N.J.

Friday, October 6, 1995
9 am Celebration of Mass at Aqueduct Racetrack, Queens, N.Y.
5 pm Evening prayer and address, St. Joseph's Seminary, Yonkers, N.Y.

Saturday, October 7, 1995
9 am Celebration of Mass at Central Park, New York, N.Y.
3:30 pm Recitation of Rosary at St. Patrick's Cathedral, New York, N.Y.

Sunday, October 8, 1995
9:50 am Arrival at Baltimore-Washington International Airport, Baltimore, Md.
10:45 am Celebration of Mass at Camden Yards
1:30 pm Parade through Baltimore
2:30 pm Lunch at Our Daily Bread
5 pm Visit to the Basilica of the Assumption
5:45 pm Visit and Address to Cathedral of Mary Our Queen
7:30 pm Departure ceremony, Baltimore-Washington International Airport

"I ... come as a pilgrim of peace."
John Paul II, Newark International Airport, October 4, 1995.

New Jersey

He had been brought here on a mission: To walk again.

If his grandmother had anything to say about it, Alexis Lawson, whose legs had been crushed under a forklift two years earlier, would be touched by the pope, then stand and walk right out of the city of Newark.

The 35-year-old man and his 65-year-old grandmother, Georgette Benissan, had arrived at the crack of dawn to stake out a spot on the sidewalk across from the Cathedral of the Sacred Heart, where Pope John Paul II was to conduct the first religious service of his five-day, four-city American tour.

Oh, they would eventually see him. But like everyone else who would wait for hours just for a fleeting glimpse of the pope, they would have to be patient. And faithful.

In a 24-hour period, the pontiff would meet with President Bill Clinton at Newark International Airport, lead a prayer service at the Newark cathedral, deliver a major address to the United Nations, celebrate Mass at Giants Stadium and greet thousands of people from behind the thick, bulletproof glass of his popemobile.

Opposite page:
Pope John Paul II smiles on the flight from Rome to the United States.
PHOTO BY DEAN CURTIS

Left:
The pope speaks to reporters on Shepherd I.
PHOTO BY DEAN CURTIS

Below:
Alitalia pilots wave American and Vatican flags from the papal plane
PHOTO BY JIM GRAHAM

Students from Roselle, N.J., snap a picture of the pope.

PHOTO BY DEAN CURTIS

It would never stop raining.

But that didn't stop followers from coming by the thousands. And thousands. Jubilant people — and so many children! — of all cultures and denominations, who sang and danced and celebrated the coming of this spiritual icon.

Some even considered the gloomy weather a gift from God, in light of a debilitating drought that was plaguing the area. On the first day, the pope, himself, hinted at as much when he stepped off "Shepherd I" at the Newark Airport into a steady, gray drizzle and proclaimed, "Pope bringing you the rain. Very important event."

So, the rain didn't matter — nothing much mattered, except that they be with him — even when they were so far away they could only

John Paul II arrives at Newark International Airport.

President and Mrs. Clinton greet the pope at Newark International Airport.

PHOTO BY JOHN SEVERSON

Students from Holy Spirit School in Union, N.J. wave papal flags.

PHOTO BY JIM GRAHAM

see him on a giant-sized video screen.

The rain certainly didn't matter to Norman Sergeant and Rocco Dante, who had practically the worst seats in the house at Giants Stadium for the pope's Mass. Hey, they said, so what? Yes, they were way up in the upper deck, where there was absolutely no protection against the slanting rain that had begun falling some five hours before the scheduled 6 p.m. start of the service. And yes, they were sitting behind the altar, meaning they'd have to spend much of the night staring up at the pope's magnified image on the scoreboard. And, no, they weren't the least bit disappointed.

"I'd just kind of like to say I was here," said Sergeant, 28, of Wayne, N.J., huddled in his seat in the upper deck. "I'm waiting to see what it is going to be like. Because this is basically a church right now, which is a little hard to fathom."

Indeed. In addition to being devout Catholics, Sergeant and Dante, 25, are season ticket holders for New York Giants football games. In fact, the two Army reserve officers could see their football seats from their perches as they settled back in camouflage rain slickers — giant hoagies tucked inside. Already, they joked about the need to make some distinctions between the stadium-turned-basilica and the one used for rollicking sporting events. "I'm a little afraid I might forget myself and yell 'Let's go,

Saddle shoes are part of the Catholic school girls' uniform.

PHOTO BY JIM GRAHAM

your holiness!' " said Sergeant.

Sergeant and Rocco are of the age group that supposedly is deserting the Catholic Church. And yet, at times, Giants Stadium appeared practically overrun by young men and women — people like Debra Holloway, 31, who won two tickets to the Mass in her church's lottery, then marched right in to her boss to ask for the day off. And she got it — no questions asked.

"Usually, you have to give a couple of weeks' notice," said Holloway, who works on Wall Street. "But when I asked, my boss said, "How could I say no?'"

Marin Diaz understands that attitude. Diaz, who arrived in Newark from Puerto Rico two weeks earlier, couldn't miss the chance to wait on the sidewalk when he learned the pope was coming to Sacred Heart Cathedral: "The whole thing gave me chills. I can't believe he is really here," Diaz said. "We came to see the pope, and we leave knowing that religion is still a major force that guides our lives."

Ebullient, despite an eight-hour flight from Rome, the pope arrived at 3:20 p.m. at Newark International Airport where he was greeted by President and Mrs. Clinton, 800 dignitaries, including New Jersey Governor Christie Whitman and New York Governor George Pataki. A huge contingent from the American Roman Catholic hierarchy included the pontiff's friends John Cardinal O'Connor from New York, William Cardinal Keeler from Baltimore and Archbishop Theodore McCarrick from Newark.

Newark Mayor Sharpe James expressed pride that his city was making history. "We have the Holy Father. We have the president. The world is here. Right here," he exclaimed.

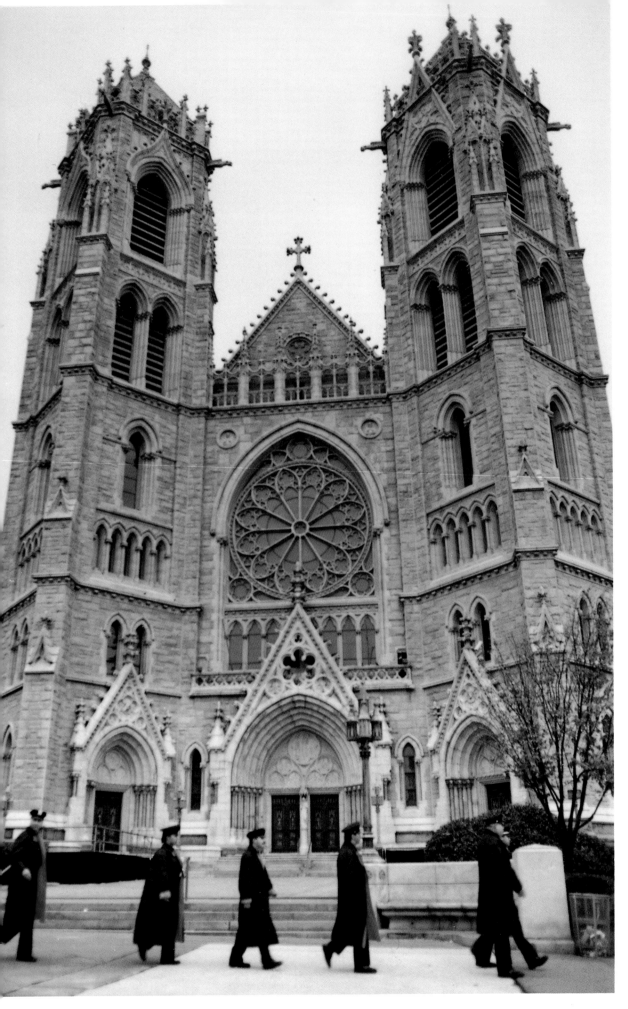

Police file past Sacred Heart Cathedral, ready to set up a security perimeter before the pope arrives.

James praised the Catholic church for staying and investing in Newark — an inner-city in peril — when so many other organizations have given up hope and fled. "The church never abandoned us," he said. "The churches, the schools, the hospitals all stayed in the neighborhoods and kept the neighborhoods together."

Euphoria quickly swept the crowd at the airport when the pope's green and white Alitalia jetliner glided into sight. Once the plane landed and the door opened to reveal the pontiff inside, 2,000 parochial school children dressed in plaid uniforms and saddle shoes roared, the West Point band played, and tears streamed down the faces of women and men, young and old.

The sound was deafening as the pontiff gingerly eased his way down the steps of the plane to

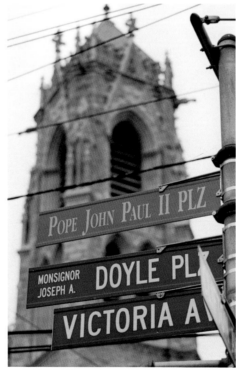

A new red street sign was added near the cathedral.

PHOTO BY DAVID BERGELAND

Early morning singers celebrate the pope's impending arrival at Sacred Heart Cathedral.

PHOTO BY J.M. EDDINS, JR.

Television reporters broadcast early morning reports from Branch Brook Park, across from Sacred Heart Cathedral.

Comedian Joe Piscopo greets fans before attending the cathedral service.

the tarmac.

"As you have clearly gathered from the welcome of the children and the not-so-young, all Americans are very, very happy to see you," President Clinton said.

The pope was clearly delighted with the reception. Then, he spoke slowly and deliberately, his image barely visible to the gathered masses over the sea of umbrellas from the VIP seats.

"It is a great joy for me to return to the United States," the pontiff said.

Just so for everyone.

Said Archbishop McCarrick, at the start of Mass at Giants Stadium the next day: "We, your family in New Jersey, rejoice as you come to lead us."

Indeed, for weeks before John Paul II arrived, the Newark Archdiocese building clamored

Security personnel check potted mums before they are taken into the cathedral.

with the excitement of a family preparing for a wedding. Hundreds of workers, many of them volunteers, prepared for the pope's visit 'round the clock, a labor of love. Most were sleep-deprived and spending days at a time away from their families. Yet their spirits soared at the near-ness of the pope's arrival.

In fact, just days before, Archdiocese spokesman Michael Hurley, who by now was substi-tuting cat naps for real sleep, predicted the visit would be, "in the words of any kid in the neigh-borhood, awesome. We can't wait."

On that first day, at Sacred Heart Cathedral, with only 1,800 seats available for the evening Vespers service, the pews were already half full three hours

A high point on the cathedral is used as a security vantage point.

The popemobile rolls down Clifton Avenue in Newark, N.J.

PHOTO BY BETH BALBIERZ

before the pope was to arrive. If anything qualified as the "cheap seats," it was a row of white folding chairs placed at the very rear of the cathedral. Anthony Conte, seated there, was unswerving in his faith that he would somehow see the pope. "I have a feeling," Conte said over and over, not daring to put into actual words his fervent hope: that the pope would bypass the doors near the High Altar and make a grand entrance through the ornate front doors just a few feet from his seat. "I just have a good feeling."

Conte was absolutely right. At 5:55 p.m. a murmur swept through the crowd and John Paul II swept through the front doors of Sacred Heart Cathedral. For the next eight minutes, he moved up the center aisle — arms outstretched — slowed by hands that reached out for him. Over and over, he allowed himself to be pulled, first this way by nuns, then that way by a priest or parishioner. All sought the same goal: a look, a touch, some connection with this most holy man. No one would walk away disappointed. Not if the pope could possibly prevent it.

Finally, he reached the

Alejandro Fernandez, 4, watches from behind the fence at his home near the cathedral.
PHOTO BY J.M. EDDINS, JR.

People crowd porches to watch the pope's arrival.

PHOTO BY DAVID BERGELAND

Photographers scurry into position as the pope arrives.

PHOTO BY WALTER CHOROSZEWSKI

front, and while much of the rest of the audience stood on pews and craned their necks to see, the pontiff engaged in quiet conversation with President and Mrs. Clinton. Then, he slowly mounted the stairs to the altar and, with cheers ringing out through the grand cathedral, he knelt and offered his blessing.

Outside in the rain, Alexis Lawson and his grandmother were watching a giant video screen to see the scene inside the cathedral. The frail man still clutched a framed picture of a relative, a bishop from Africa who had died violently there a year earlier. His grandmother stood next to his wheelchair. Lawson cried, but his tears no longer were tears of despair. He had been blessed.

Moments earlier, as the dark sky threatened to cancel the pope's procession on the streets surrounding Sacred Heart, Alexis and his grandmother were being jammed ever-tighter into the metal barricade that would separate them from the pontiff. It seemed as though the Holy Father would never be able to spot Alexis, lost in the sea of people that had formed all around him, lost in his quest for hope.

Then — like that! — John Paul II was there.

As the crowd cheered, the popemobile rounded the corner behind the cathedral and headed, ever so slowly, toward the spot where Alexis and his grandmother prayed.

As the pontiff neared — smiling, waving, nodding his head — Alexis, tears running down his cheeks, thrust the picture skyward and

People line the street to get a glimpse of the pope.

PHOTO BY DEAN CURTIS

Pope John Paul II waves from the popemobile as he arrives at Sacred Heart Cathedral.
PHOTO BY BETH BALBIERZ

Nuns greet the Holy Father as he enters the cathedral. "Touch my hand," they implored him.

PHOTO BY LOREN FISHER

President Clinton greets the pope inside the cathedral as Newark Archbishop Theodore McCarrick smiles.

PHOTO BY LOREN FISHER

Opposite page:
Pope John Paul II walks towards the Sacred Heart Cathedral altar.

PHOTO BY ALAN PETERSIME

Previous pages:
Pope John Paul II greets members of the Sacred Heart Cathedral choir.

PHOTO BY ALAN PETERSIME AND LOREN FISHER

Newark Archbishop Theodore McCarrick addresses the pontiff.

PHOTO BY CARL WALSH

Pope John Paul II gives Newark Archbishop Theodore McCarrick a hug.

PHOTO BY LOREN FISHER

smiled for the first time that day.

The pope glanced at the photograph, then down at Alexis. As their eyes locked, the Holy Father nodded, smiled and blessed Alexis with the sign of the cross.

People all around him collapsed in sobs and hugged Alexis, but he couldn't stop smiling.

"I am blessed," Alexis said. "I feel so happy. Now I want to live again."

• • •

Sacred Heart Cathedral's pews are jam-packed with people waiting to see the pope.

Photo by Alan Petersime

Prolife Anderson, of Reno, Nev., kneels in Sacred Heart Cathedral after the pontiff left. Anderson had his name legally changed to Prolife because of his strong beliefs. "He's my idol. I'd die for him," Anderson said of the pope.

PHOTO BY LOREN FISHER

Six-year-old Kaitlin Moore of Holy Innocence School in Neptune, N.J., looks out the rain-splattered bus window as she approaches Giants Stadium.

PHOTO BY BETH BALBIERZ

People weather the rain to get to Giants Stadium.

PHOTO BY JOHN SEVERSON

Giants Stadium's circular ramps are crowded with people entering the stadium to attend Mass with the pontiff.

PHOTO BY JOHN SEVERSON

Left: Mary and Frank Ziarkowski, of Somerset, N.J., get their tickets before boarding the bus at their church for Giants Stadium.
Below: On the bus, Richard Attanafio reads about the papal visit while heading to the stadium.
Bottom: At the stadium, Mary Ziarkowski sings during Mass .

PHOTOS BY BETH BALBIERZ

Opposite page:
The Giants Stadium crowd cheers the Holy Father as he passes in the pope-mobile.

PHOTO BY LOREN FISHER

Previous pages:
The pope tours Giants Stadium in the popemobile.
PHOTO BY JIM GRAHAM

Next page:
An electronic sign welcomes the pope from high above the large altar built for the event.
PHOTO BY LOREN FISHER

Pope John Paul II during Mass at Giants Stadium.
PHOTO BY LOREN FISHER

The Giants Stadium crowd came prepared for the slanting rain that pelted the stadium during the Mass.

Above:
Although soaked
by the steady rain,
a man worships.
PHOTO BY DAVID
BERGELAND

It was, after all,
Giants Stadium.
Football rain gear
helped keep wor-
shippers dry.
PHOTO BY LOREN
FISHER

Being in the presence of the pope is inspiring for people of all ages.
PHOTO BY LOREN FISHER

A priest takes a picture of the pope on the altar.
PHOTO BY DAVID BERGELAND

Covered with plastic rain gear, a spectator watches the mass using binoculars.

PHOTO BY JIM GRAHAM

A large video screen enables people in the back of the stadium to see what is happening.

PHOTO BY JOHN SEVERSON

A woman holds her rosary beads.

The crowd jumps to their feet as "the wave" goes around the stadium.

Crowds stand behind barricades waiting for the pope's arrival at the United Nations.

PHOTO BY J.M. EDDINS, JR.

"I can hardly believe we are not back in Denver, which was such an enriching experience ... I know this is not Denver. This is New York! The great, great New York!
Paul John II, Central Park, October 7, 1995

New York

It is a notoriously tough crowd to please.

Yet for 89 hours, New Yorkers embraced Pope John Paul II like almost no other figure — public or private — appearing in their midst in recent memory.

Maybe it helped that he spoke their language. Asked to address the United Nations as part of its 50th anniversary celebration, the pope more than obliged. Before him, no one had ever spoken to the General Assembly of the United Nations in all six of its official languages — without the help of a translator.

Or maybe it was that he practiced what he

preached. Just hours after imploring worshippers in Central Park to cast away their fears — "Do not be afraid! God is with you!" — the pope broke from his bodyguards and, with John Cardinal O'Connor, took to the streets around the majestic St. Patrick's Cathedral to greet the throngs who gathered there. Yes, it was a security nightmare for the battalion of Secret Service agents

and New York police who panicked every time the pontiff rolled down a window on the popemobile. But it was a dream come true for the people he touched — on the shoulder, on the forehead, deep within their souls.

Nor did it hurt that John Paul II, during Mass in Central Park, would, with unabashed fervor, break into a Polish folk song he had learned as a child. The pontiff thrilled his audience when he serenaded them with the impromptu Christmas song. "You're applauding, but you do not understand that," the grinning pope responded to his cheering congregation. They then returned the gesture, singing Silent Night to him for his "Christmas present in October."

And nearly everywhere in New York the 75-year-old pontiff went — from the United Nations to Aqueduct Racetrack to St. Joseph's Seminary, Central Park and St. Patrick's Cathedral — people marveled over his seeming tirelessness.

"He got off the plane, he met with the president, he went to the U.N., tomorrow he says Mass in Central Park... I'm exhausted just watching him on TV," said 58-year-old Claire D'Antuono, who rested wearily on her front lawn, about a half-mile from St. Joseph's Seminary, where seminarians chanted "John Paul II, we love you!"

At the United Nations, his inaugural New York engagement, the pope delivered a rousing address and challenged nations

Above: The pope accepts flowers from children in the U.N. General Assembly.
PHOTO BY DEAN CURTIS

Right: The children's choir from the U. N. International School perform.
PHOTO BY DEAN CURTIS

The pontiff tours the U.N. with Secretary General Boutros Boutros-Ghali, left.

PHOTO BY DEAN CURTIS

to confront their moral crises and strive for diversity and harmony.

As he spoke, pockets of people waited outside the U.N., though a steady rain kept the crowd relatively small. Those who did endure were a spirited bunch. From pupils and their teachers, to businessmen and women, grandmothers and protesters, they sang, chanted, marched and cheered. Some — people who claimed title to everything from atheists to aliens to anti-meat eaters — carried placards touting their causes.

Most of the spectators were just hoping to steal a glance at their spiritual leader.

The next day, for the first time during the visit of John Paul II, the sun finally shone.

Pope John Paul II speaks to the General Assembly of the United Nations.

PHOTO BY DEAN CURTIS

The pope delivers his address to the General Assembly.

PHOTO BY DEAN CURTIS

An estimated 75,000 people jammed into the stands and spilled over into seats set up for the Mass at Aqueduct Racetrack. Some began lining up as early as 2 a.m. But closer to the pope's 9 a.m. scheduled arrival time, gridlock outside the racetrack caused feelings of trepidation for the hundreds of people stuck in buses transporting them to the Mass. Some were visibly shaken by the long delays, fearful they might miss what many people considered to be the most important and exciting day of their lives.

Eventually, everyone did make it into the racetrack — no matter what it took to get there.

Eileen Maza had been confined to her Queens home for two weeks prior to the pope's Aqueduct Mass. Sickly and crying, she looked up from her wheelchair outside the racetrack and said: "You see how I came. And still, no one was going to stop me. I'm so glad I made it. It was worth everything to me. Everything."

The Central Park Mass, the next day, was the largest event on the pope's American agenda. For many, this celebration also was the emotional crescendo of the five-day visit, perhaps because the pope seemed so relaxed. So human.

Five hours before the Mass was scheduled to start on Oct. 7, people began lining up outside the 50-acre Great Lawn, at the center of Central Park, and streaming into the North Meadow, where giant video screens were set up. By 6:30 a.m., buses stretched as far as the eye could see. Worshippers by the tens of thousands slogged toward the muddy park wearing rain gear and boots and carrying blankets. Hawkers pushed pope t-shirts, pope pictures, pope buttons, disposable cameras, and rosary beads that glowed in the dark. The North

Spectators wait for the pope to depart the U.N. Behind them is a large banner brought by the crowd.

A U.N. staff member watches the address on a monitor.

PHOTO BY DEAN CURTIS

Meadow had its own souvenir tents, where $3 commemorative bottled water was selling fast. "I think a lot of people are buying it so that, when the pope gives his blessing, it will become holy water," confided one vendor.

The crowds peered with wide-eyed awe at the glittering purple, gold and white altar from which the pontiff would soon celebrate Mass for the tens of thousands who were there; the millions more who watched on their television sets at home.

The crowd cheered wildly when the pope arrived shortly after 9 a.m. in his popemobile. The 2-1/2 hour service that followed was both festive and solemn, with the pope exhorting his followers to stand up for marriage and family life, to oppose abortion, to aid the poor, the hungry and the homeless, and to care for the sick, including people with AIDS.

Police estimated the crowd on the Great Lawn alone at more than 125,000 people. They were followers of all ages and backgrounds. And they shared a spirit of camaraderie that is seldom found in large crowds, particularly in New York. No pushing or shoving, no angry exchanges. Instead, happy people chanting, cheering, singing and praying.

They also shared a spirit of youth, one which the

The subway is crowded near Aqueduct Racetrack.

PHOTO BY DAVID BERGELAND

Previous pages:
The sun starts to rise on Aqueduct Racetrack.
PHOTO BY WALTER CHOROSZEWSKI

A sign points the way to tickets at Aqueduct Racetrack.
PHOTO BY DAVID BERGELAND

pope himself recognized. John Paul II compared the gathering to the one he hosted on World Youth Day in Denver two years before.

"So many thousands of young people astonished everyone with their spirit and their faith," the pontiff said. "I remember clearly that many, many people wondered and worried that the young people of America would not come to the World Youth Day, or, if they did come, that they would be a problem. Instead the young people's joy, their hunger for the truth, their desire to be united all together in the body of Christ, made clear to everyone that many, very many young people of America, have values and ideals which seldom make the headlines. Is it any wonder that the pope loves you?"

The crowd roared.

MTV's Alison Stewart was among them. "It's a big cultural event," she said. "Some young people are more spiritual than people give them credit for."

Within a few hours, 3,000 worshippers at St. Patrick's Cathedral would be equally jubilant when John Paul II led them in the rosary.

Ticket takers have their hands full at the gate.

Photo by Walter Choroszewski

People and buses line up near the racetrack.

Photo by David Bergeland

The pope lands at Aqueduct Racetrack aboard a U.S. Marine Blackhawk helicopter.

People hold up signs saying "We Love You Papa."

During the service, the pontiff drew zealous applause when he invoked the familiar credo, "The family that prays together stays together."

The streets outside St. Patrick's were jammed with onlookers who craned their necks to watch the pontiff on giant video screens. Some even climbed poles to get a better look.

No one expected what was about to happen: that they would meet John Paul II face-to-face. In an extraordinary move, after the service the pontiff left the cathedral and, instead of heading for his limousine, walked out onto Fifth Avenue to greet the crowd.

"He's walking!" someone shouted. "He's walking!"

The pontiff kissed heads, held hands and touched shoulders. It was as if he needed to feel the people of this city he had called great.

In turn, throughout his visit, New York seemed to take on some of the goodness of the pope.

Witness the story of Kathleen Brady, an elderly lady who had traveled to New York all the way from West Palm Beach to see John Paul II.

"I don't have a ticket," she sobbed outside Aqueduct Racetrack. "This is my old neighborhood. I just want to see the pope in my old neighborhood."

Many days in New York, a weeping woman elicits little notice. But this was a day celebrating the human spirit.

Just after John Paul II arrived at the racetrack, a kindly policeman escorted the old woman to a seat he had found for her inside.

"This is such a beautiful time," the old woman cried.

• • •

Worshippers raise
their hands in
praise as the
pope arrives.
PHOTO BY DEAN
CURTIS

The pope greets the crowd as he walks onto the Aqueduct Racetrack altar.

PHOTO BY DEAN CURTIS

The crowd waves to the pope.

PHOTO BY DEAN CURTIS

The pope serves communion to a young girl.

PHOTO BY DEAN CURTIS

Priests give communion in front of the grandstand.

PHOTO BY WALTER CHOROSZEWSKI

Winnie M. Callejo, of Flushing, N.Y., holds a crucifix outside the racetrack.

PHOTO BY DAVID BERGELAND

People kneel and pray during Mass at Aqueduct Racetrack.

PHOTO BY WALTER CHOROSZEWSKI

Jennifer Mack, 10, of Flemington, N.J., and her sister, Alyson, 7, watch the pope on TV at a Nobody Beats The Wiz store in Raritan, N.J.

PHOTO BY ED MURRAY

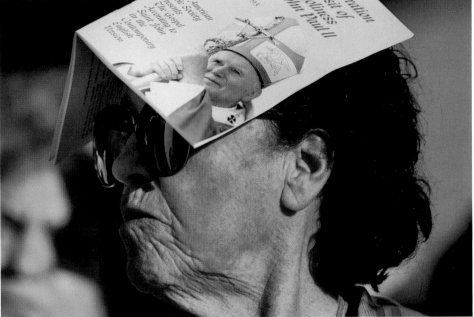

Alice Sullivan of Mastic Beach, N.Y., shields her eyes from the sun.

PHOTO BY CARL WALSH

CELEBRATION OF THE EUCHARIST
OCTOBER 6, 1995 - 9:30 A.M.
AQUEDUCT RACE TRACK

A member of the Knights of Columbus holds his ticket to the pope's Mass at Aqueduct. The Knights of Columbus were one of the sponsors for the Aqueduct visit.

PHOTO BY WALTER CHOROSZEWSKI

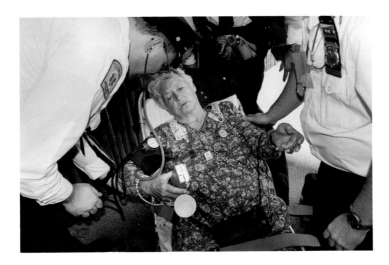

Kathleen Brady gets help from emergency medical personnel but refused to go to the hospital.

PHOTO BY J.M. EDDINS, JR.

Thousands of folding chairs were set up between the grandstand and the altar.

PHOTO BY WALTER CHOROSZEWSKI

Security personnel walk with the popemobile through St. Joseph's Seminary.

PHOTO BY JOHN SEVERSON

The crowd cheers the pope's arrival at the seminary.

PHOTO BY JOHN SEVERSON

Virginia Piccini of Hartsdale, N.Y., is overcome with emotion as the pontiff passes in the popemobile.

Even a New York City police detective needs papal credentials.

Nuns get ready to take snapshots of the pope.

The Holy Father is greeted on the steps of the seminary.

Photo by Dean Curtis

The pope reads during the service.

PHOTO BY DEAN CURTIS

Linda Milagros, of Yonkers, watches the pope on a large video screen and offers an icon to be blessed. At left is her friend, Ann Russo of Conn.

PHOTO BY JOHN SEVERSON

The crowd waits to get into Central Park's Great Lawn before the sun comes up.

PHOTO BY DAVID BERGELAND

Local TV crews get ready for their morning reports.

PHOTO BY ALAN PETERSIME

People wait in
Central Park for
the Mass to begin.
Photo by John
Severson

The crowd waits to get into Central Park.

Photo by Carl Walsh

A heated debate rages outside the park.

The pope arrives at the large stage built in Central Park.

PHOTO BY DEAN CURTIS

Right: People in the back of the crowd wave flags.

PHOTO BY DAVID BERGELAND

Below: The New York City skyline looms over the Central Park crowd.

PHOTO BY LOREN FISHER

Jojo and Divine Chua sing during the Mass.

The Holy Father
celebrates Mass
at Central Park.
PHOTO BY DEAN
CURTIS

Above: Rose Catalano, 83, of Staten Island, N.Y., listens intently to the words of the pope.

PHOTO BY LOREN FISHER

A child sitting with priests loses interest in the service.

PHOTO BY DEAN CURTIS

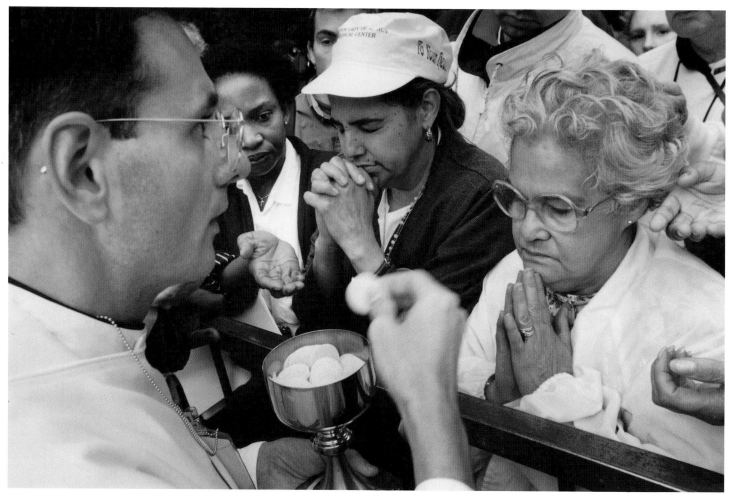

Father Rick Mickey, of Memphis, Tenn., gives communion.

Right: One man gets the duty of taking a group's picture with several cameras from the group.

PHOTO BY J.M. EDDINS, JR.

Above, Lisa Cournoyer, of Rhode Island, Breeda Connolly of New York and Cindy Minon of Arizona, hug after the Central Park Mass. Lisa and Breeda came to the park together and met Cindy while waiting in line. They became friends during their short time together.

PHOTO BY LOREN FISHER

Carmen Ramos, of Huntington Station, N.Y., shows two women a ceramic statue she brought to Central Park.

PHOTO BY LOREN FISHER

T-shirts of all kinds are hawked to people leaving the park.

PHOTO BY DAVID BERGELAND

Mary Walsh, of Babylon, N.Y., and Cecila Maher, of Ireland, carry photos of the pope they bought while leaving the park.

A large crowd gathers outside St. Patrick's Cathedral as a large video screen shows the worship service that is taking place inside.

PHOTO BY JOHN SEVERSON

Pope John Paul II recites the rosary during the service in St. Patrick's Cathedral.

New York City policemen cut down a street sign in front of St. Patrick's Cathedral.

The pope takes a tour of the area around the cathedral.

PHOTO BY BETH BALBIERZ

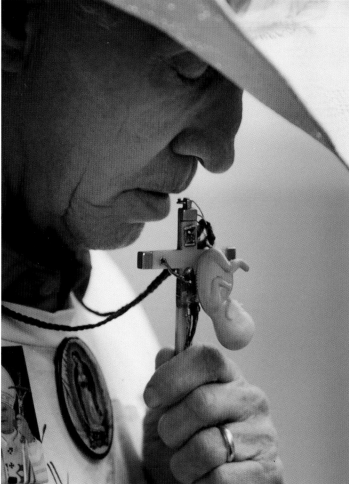

A man prays with a cross that has a fetus on it.

PHOTO BY DEAN CURTIS

A woman holds her rosary while waiting to get a glimpse of the pope.
PHOTO BY BETH BALBIERZ

"Since the beginning of my papal ministry, I have repeatedly affirmed the importance of social solidarity as an instrument for building up the civilization of love for which humanity yearns."

John Paul II, Camden Yards, October 8, 1995.

Maryland

One day after celebrating Mass for several hundred thousand in a massive outdoor cathedral otherwise known as Central Park, Pope John Paul II broke bread with fewer than two dozen Maryland Catholics in a humble soup kitchen in Baltimore.

The meal was simple, the utensils were plastic, and the conversation centered around kids and school. On this, the final leg of a jam-packed, five-day itinerary, the pope seemed a bit weary as he sat down to a lunch of chicken and rice casserole, peas and carrots. But he also seemed at ease in the soup kitchen, perhaps the most intimate engagement of his ambitious American tour.

Seven of the invited guests were children, and he reveled in their company. Upon meeting 5-year-old Julio Damian, the pontiff seemed more like a loving grandfather than influential world leader when he reached down and gently tweaked the boy's nose.

Sister Paula Laschenski stared almost wonderingly at the remains of lunch, once the pope had gone: a crumpled paper napkin and a half-eaten roll, a melted puddle of vanilla ice cream in a simple brown plastic bowl.

A pilot waves the Vatican flag out the window of "Shepherd I" as the papal plane taxis at Baltimore-Washington International Airport.

PHOTO BY ALAN PETERSIME

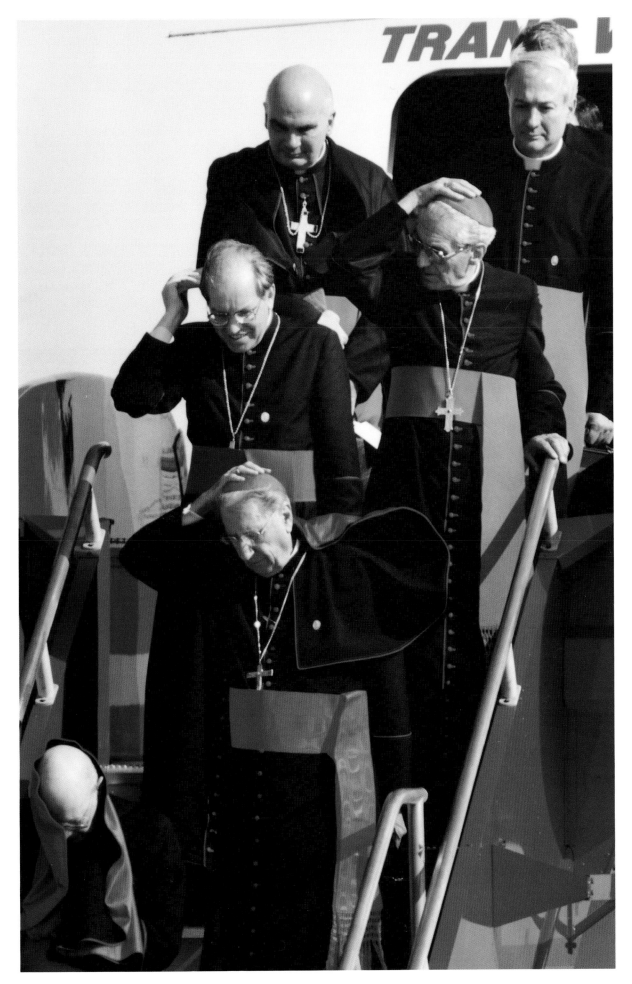

Some of the papal party depart the plane in Baltimore.
PHOTO BY JIM GRAHAM

The pope hugs Melissa Brent, left, and Justin Farinelli, who presented him flowers at the airport.

PHOTO BY BETH BALBIERZ

The flight crew takes pictures after the pope has left the plane.
PHOTO BY JIM GRAHAM

"We're having trouble even moving the things at his place," she said. "It's like it's sacred."

The pope had saved the first for last when he chose to end his American visit in Baltimore. Baltimore was the first Roman Catholic diocese in America. Since it was formed more than 200 years ago, it has established a long list of firsts: First to elect an American bishop. First to form an American seminary and an American convent. First to build an American cathedral.

In the eyes of all Baltimore, the pope also saved the best for last. Certainly, it was the day that gave a special, human dimension to a tour noted for its breadth and grandeur.

The sun had barely risen when crowds began gathering anywhere the Pope was scheduled to make even the briefest appearance. At Baltimore-Washington International Airport, a hundred diplomats and their families huddled together in a small reception area, waiting for "Shepherd I." Downtown, spectators by the thousands lined Pratt Street to view what was to be the first-ever papal parade, one complete with marching bands, bagpipers and children dressed in colorful costumes. Nearby, Camden Yards stood

Left: The sun shines brightly on the hands of Baltimore's William Cardinal Keeler.

PHOTO BY JIM GRAHAM

Bus traffic makes its way to Camden Yards.

PHOTO BY CARL WALSH

Brittany Smith, 5, of Baltimore holds up a sign to get tickets to see the pope.

PHOTO BY J.M. EDDINS, JR.

ready to receive the tens of thousands more who would witness Maryland's first papal Mass.

When John Paul II finally stepped off "Shepherd I" in Baltimore at 10:13 a.m. on Oct. 8, his gait was slow, but deliberate and steady. For the first time since he arrived in America, he was late — probably because he had spent so much time at Newark Airport, thanking police officers and black-jumpsuited army guards who had accompanied him in the New York area.

Despite his seeming fatigue, the pontiff was obviously delighted, and perhaps even drew a little strength from two small children who handed him flowers, then were unexpectedly pulled into a papal embrace. The pope's eyes

Cardinals and other officials make their way to the altar before the pope arrives at Camden Yards.

The baseball field is filled with celebrants before the Mass begins.

The pope's motor-cade winds through downtown Baltimore.

Photo by Carl Walsh

A nun becomes emotional when the Holy Father enters the stadium.
PHOTO BY LOREN FISHER

sparkled and his pink cheeks seemed even more flushed against the brilliant blue sky. With his white cassock snapping in the breeze, he faced the cheering crowd and waved. At the bottom of the stairs, William Cardinal Keeler knelt and kissed the pontiff's ring.

If John Paul II was beaming at that point, the city of Baltimore shined even brighter on this heavenly, summer-like day. For the first time since he arrived on a raw, gray day in New Jersey, the weather was perfect.

Within moments of the pope's arrival at the airport, he was on the move again, headed for Camden Yards where a record crowd of 50,000 had gathered to celebrate Mass.

"He is here." The words flash on the scoreboard as the pope tours the stadium.
PHOTO BY LOREN FISHER

People line up for communion.
PHOTO BY LOREN FISHER

Opposite page: A photo of the pope is projected on the stadium scoreboard.
PHOTO BY LOREN FISHER

Right: Communion is given to people outside the stadium.
PHOTO BY CARL WALSH

"He Is Coming." The words flashed on the scoreboard as images of the pope's motorcade speeding toward the ballpark played out on the center field video screen. People chanted, cheered and danced. Some wiped away tears. The choir led a rousing rendition of "Halle, Halle, Halle, Luja."

Religious recording artist Michael W. Smith had just finished serenading the crowd. He described the scene in Camden Yards this way: "Out of control — in a godly way."

Then ... "He is Here."

It was 10:55 a.m. The pontiff appeared suddenly from the right-field gate, sitting high in the sparkling white popemobile. While the pop singing group Boyz II Men sang a cappella, the pope circled the ballpark slowly, waving, nodding, blessing the crowd with the sign of the cross.

"There he is!" "It's him!" "It's really him."

A sea of tiny yellow and red

A large cross dominates the altar.

A bald head makes a good place to display greetings.

Right: Pope John Paul II during Mass at Camden Yards.

Pope John Paul II waves from the altar. Beside him is Msgr. Piero Marini, Master of Liturgical Celebrations.

papal flags waved and people stood on their seats, hoping for a better look. But this crowd seemed somehow different from other large crowds the pope had presided over during his American visit. They were more constrained, perhaps more prayerful, too. Yet they were no less moved by the pope's presence.

As the pope arrived, neighbors clasped hands and sang hymns. Strangers prayed with strangers. An elderly mother and her grown son embraced and sobbed. And, even though logic told them the pontiff was too far away to touch, that didn't stop them from reaching out to him anyway.

Jack Mitchell slumped in his seat, ran a hand through his salt-and-pepper hair, then dabbed at tears after the pope passed.

"He blessed me," he said. "I'm sure he blessed me."

So many were blessed. Blessed in ways that will endure longer

Above, the enthusiastic crowd cheers the pope as he leaves the ballpark.
PHOTO BY WALTER CHOROSZEWSKI

Left: A celebrant dressed in traditional Peruvian clothing enjoys the day.
PHOTO BY DEAN CURTIS

People wait for the pope at Harbor Place in downtown Baltimore.

PHOTO BY JOHN SEVERSON

The Secret Service checks manholes before the parade begins.

PHOTO BY JOHN SEVERSON

The papal parade leaves from Camden Yards and heads down Pratt Street.

PHOTO BY CARL WALSH

A marching band adds color to the parade through the streets of downtown Baltimore.

PHOTO BY JIM GRAHAM

Opposite page:
The parade heads up Light Street.

PHOTO BY JESSE MAY

People on a balcony applaud the parade as it passes under them.

PHOTO BY J.M. EDDINS, JR.

Above: The Secret Service escorts the pope-mobile on the parade route.

Photo by John Severson

Angele Loner, of Logansport, Ind., shades her eyes from the sun.

Photo by John Severson

Barbara Pudlo, of Manchester, N.H., cries when the pope passes.

PHOTO BY BETH BALBIERZ

than the memory of a simple gesture.

Outside Camden Yards, crowds ten people deep lined the mile-long papal parade route. Many rejoiced to know that soon it would be their turn to see John Paul II. The atmosphere in downtown Baltimore was more like a street fair than a religious event. Music blared, and the scent of warm pretzels and roasting chestnuts wafted through the air. Street vendors peddled everything from pope t-shirts, baseball caps and buttons, to pope phone cards, magnets, key chains, bumper stickers and towels. There were even pope tattoos. Judy Buck-Kennedy wore hers on her cheek. "The pope's cool," she said. "He's Polish and I'm Polish."

The parade had all the trap-

Pope tattoos added to the fun of the parade and celebration.

PHOTO BY JOHN SEVERSON

Souvenir buttons are sold on the Baltimore parade route.

A man wears a t-shirt created by a Baltimore radio station
Photo by J.M. Eddins, Jr.

pings of a homecoming celebration for an adopted hero: marching bands strutting their stuff; costumed children waving banners; bagpipers wailing their distinctive welcome.

Emotions soared wherever the pope went.

Police officers assigned to the parade route wiped away tears at the sight of him. At the soup kitchen, tight lipped Secret Service agents looked like naughty school children as they giddily snapped each others' photos posing by the popemobile. At the Basilica of the Assumption, where the pontiff stopped briefly after his lunch at the soup kitchen, guests dropped to their knees to kiss his ring.

At the Cathedral of Mary Our Queen, 13-year-old Katelyn Hoffman was among 1,300 guests invited for the pope's final prayer service. Katelyn had prayed for an aisle seat, but she hadn't expected a miracle.

The eighth grader said she noticed the pope glance her way

For some, climbing a tree proved to be the best vantage point for watching the parade.
Photo by Beth Balbierz

Above: Lunch at Our Daily Bread soup kitchen.
PHOTO BY ALAN PETERSIME

Left: The pope gets ready to give Brittany Campbell a kiss after lunch.
PHOTO BY ALAN PETERSIME

Brittany Campbell gives the pope a hug after lunch at Our Daily Bread soup kitchen.

PHOTO BY ALAN PETERSIME

Secret Service agents have their picture taken in front of the popemobile as it sits outside the soup kitchen.

Photo by Alan Petersime

as he headed down the aisle after the prayer service. As people all around her — people her parents' and grandparents' ages — stood on pews reaching for him and shouting "Papa!" "Papa!", Katelyn stood frozen as the pontiff approached.

"First he held my hand, and then he patted my shoulder and hugged me," she said afterward, as she sat on a pew, her face flushed red, trying to catch her breath.

"I couldn't do anything," Katelyn said. "This is the most exciting thing that has ever happened to me. I'll remember it for my whole life."

As extraordinary as Katelyn's experience was, it was almost typical of five glorious days in October — five days when, from New Jersey to New York to Baltimore, adults behaved like awestruck children and children caught a glimpse of an ageless faith as they beheld one of the spiritual leaders of our time.

Said Debra Hollaway, who thought nothing of waiting five hours to claim some of the worst seating in rain-soaked Giants Stadium in New Jersey, "This is probably the closest we'll ever get to God."

• • •

A little boy is
amazed to meet
the pope.
PHOTO BY ALAN
PETERSIME

The pope takes in the view outside the basilica.

Left: The dome of the basilica glows
before the pope arrives.

Sister Edita and
Sister Aubrey from
St. Joseph's Villa
in Emittsburg, Md.
cross themselves
during the service
at Cathedral of
Mary Our Queen.
PHOTO BY LOREN
FISHER

Pope John Paul II prays at one of the small chapels at The Cathedral of Mary Our Queen.

PHOTO BY LOREN FISHER

Becky Mitchell, 9, Meghan Wagner, 10, and Amanda Bory, 8, practice the Star Spangled Banner they will perform in sign for the pope.

PHOTO BY DAVID BERGELAND

Pope John Paul II listens to the speech given by Vice-President Al Gore during departure ceremonies at the airport.

Photo by Beth Balbierz

Right: The pope waves goodbye as he gets ready to return to Rome.
PHOTO BY BETH BALBIERZ

The pope and Vice-President Al Gore walk toward the airport podium.

PHOTO BY DAVID BERGELAND

A band sits ready to play as the pope gives his farewell address.

PHOTO BY ALAN PETERSIME

Prints available

The Jersey Photographic Project and Elf Publishing, Inc. are offering five 8X10 color glossy photos of the historic papal trip. Each photo is hand printed and suitable for framing.

The photos are only $25 each or $100 for all five plus $4.00 shipping and handling for each order. Photos will be delivered within one week of receiving the order.

For credit card orders only, call 1-800-999-2266

Mail check or money orders to:

Elf Publishing, Inc.,

P.O. Box 15275, Fort Wayne, IN 46885-5275

Be sure to include:

• Letter and name of photos wanted

• Check or money order for $25 for each photo or $100 for all five plus $4.00 shipping and handling for each order.

• Your name and address

Photo A - Giants Stadium

Photo B - Hugging kids

Photo C - Holding staff

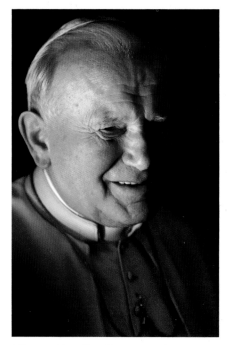
Photo D - Smiling on airplane

Photo E - Basilica of the Assumption